T0311338

365 Quotes for Teachers

Start your morning with a daily dose of inspiration! Bestselling author Danny Steele, known for his motivational @steelethoughts tweets, brings you a powerful quote for every day of the year.

You'll find quotes on topics such as reaching your students, working with colleagues, taking care of yourself, remembering your purpose, and more.

Read them to kick off your morning, to wind down at night, or whenever you need to recharge. The uplifting, insightful quotes will remind you of the positive impact you're having on your students, each and every day.

Danny Steele (@steelethoughts) is a principal from Birmingham, Alabama, and has worked in public education for over 28 years. In 2016, he was named Alabama's Secondary Principal of the Year. He has presented at numerous state and national conferences and writes an educational leadership blog that has received over 5 million page views.

365 Quotes for Teachers

Inspiration and Motivation for
Every Day of the Year

Danny Steele

Routledge
Taylor & Francis Group

NEW YORK AND LONDON

First published 2022
by Routledge
605 Third Avenue, New York, NY 10158

and by Routledge
2 Park Square, Milton Park, Abingdon, Oxon, OX14 4RN

Routledge is an imprint of the Taylor & Francis Group, an informa business

Library of Congress Cataloging-in-Publication Data
A catalog record for this title has been requested

ISBN: 978-1-032-10754-7 (hbk)
ISBN: 978-1-032-07635-5 (pbk)
ISBN: 978-1-003-21688-9 (ebk)

DOI: 10.4324/9781003216889

Typeset in Palatino
by Apex CoVantage, LLC

Contents

Acknowledgements

With every project, there are important individuals to acknowledge. This book would not have happened if my brother, David, hadn't encouraged me to begin networking with other educators. Engaging with other professionals on social media has transformed my career. I could not ask for a more supportive editor. I'm grateful to Lauren Davis and her team at Routledge for believing in my message and supporting this project. I'm grateful to all the educators out there with whom I have connected on social media. There are too many of you to mention, but thank you for engaging. Thank you for supporting me, and thank you for sharing my thoughts over the years. And to my wife, Holley . . . thank you for being so patient with me as I navigated the "Twitterverse." You have my gratitude; you have my respect; and you have my heart.

Meet the Author

Dr. Danny Steele is a principal from Birmingham, Alabama, and has worked in public education for over 28 years. In addition to serving as a principal at multiple levels, he has worked as a teacher, coach, assistant principal, and university instructor. In 2005, Danny was recognized as the Secondary Assistant Principal of the Year for the state of Alabama, and in 2016, he was named Alabama's Secondary Principal of the Year. He has presented at numerous state and national conferences, and he writes an educational leadership blog that has received over 5 million page views. Danny has an undergraduate degree in History from Covenant College (Lookout Mountain, Georgia); he has a graduate degree in History from the University of Alabama, Birmingham; he has an Educational Specialist degree in Educational Administration and an Educational Doctorate degree in Educational Leadership—both from Samford University (Birmingham, Alabama). He lives with his wife, Holley, in Birmingham, Alabama. They have three children; DJ, Will, and Elizabeth.

Introduction

I first started sharing my educational thoughts on Twitter about five years ago. I quickly realized there are thousands of educators out there who appreciate being validated in their own beliefs about education. They appreciate being reminded of their purpose. And so my journey began . . . tweeting about the core values that drive teachers. The quotes in this book are drawn from that journey. Quotes can serve as guideposts as you navigate the challenges in your career. They can crystalize your thoughts; they can underscore your values; and they can clarify your priorities. It is my hope that you will see yourselves in these pages—that you will be reconnected to the heart of teaching—that you will feel supported and encouraged to continue in your noble profession. These quotes are meant to motivate you, to challenge you, and to help you keep your job in perspective. I hope you enjoy them. I hope they nourish your "teacher soul."

365 Quotes

1

~~~~~~~~

There are a number of qualities that define effective teachers, but one that stands out to me is this: teachers are enjoying their own lesson and they're enjoying the students they're teaching.

DOI: 10.4324/9781003216889-2

2

~~~~~~~~

Learning is voluntary. That's a sobering thought when you consider it. So your goal is to create a classroom environment where the students think the learning is worth the effort and worth the risk.

3

~~~~~~~~

Effective teachers are not just "gifted educators." They work hard to plan meaningful lessons. They work hard to connect with their students and inspire them. Their level of commitment always matters.

4

~~~~~~

Positive teachers don't just make a difference in their classroom . . . they make a difference in their school's culture.

5

~~~~~~

Inspiration does not need to be a fleeting feeling. I think an inspired teacher is a teacher who comes to work every day mindful of their true purpose. And that ultimate purpose is not found in their lesson; it is found in the students they are teaching.

6

There are some teachers who are tired, stressed, and just trying to make it through their day. And some students are too.

7

Being an effective teacher is not primarily about being nice, having the right personality, having good relationships with students, having a positive attitude, or even loving the kids. It's about ensuring students learn at high levels. You can't ever forget that. It's about the learning.

8

There is very little that can replace a teacher who is excited about their lesson.

9

Teachers, you are not ultimately responsible for the success of your students. But the research is clear: you ARE a crucial variable. There are times when your initiative, your compassion, and your perseverance give students the hope and the ability to keep pushing.

10

~~~~~

When you have a difficult, disrespectful, and defiant student, my biggest tip for you . . . is to have lots of conversations with them when they are not in trouble. These conversations are where you build rapport . . . and that rapport makes future confrontations less likely.

11

~~~~~

I don't think teachers will be remembered primarily for their lessons. I think they will be remembered for their energy . . . their attitude . . . and their relationships. Lessons are important . . . but they don't tell the entire story. The legacy of a teacher is more than that.

12

Students want to be seen. They want to matter. Teachers do more than just teach academic standards; they bring hope. They're not just preparing students for the next grade level; they're preparing them for life.

13

One of the best things an educator can do in the course of the day is to have a conversation with a student about something other than school.

14

I think it's important for us to assume that students want to succeed. I think when we give them the benefit of the doubt, it makes it more likely that they will rise to our expectation. I could be wrong; I just don't think many humans enjoy failing.

15

If you want students to take an interest in your class, start by taking an interest in them.

16

~~~~~~

Students usually have better attitudes about the class when their teacher likes them. When students feel valued and respected, things run much smoother. Creating a positive class climate is actually not that complicated.

17

~~~~~~

Students might not remember what you taught them. They will always remember if you enjoyed teaching them.

18

~~~~~

Kids pick up on more than we realize. They will notice our mood . . . whether it's a good one or a bad one. And they will notice our example . . . whether it's a good one or a bad one.

19

~~~~~

Sometimes students need great role models more than they need great instructors. Teachers should never lose sight of the fact that their impact on kids often transcends the lesson.

20

Students will often become disrespectful if you embarrass them. And they won't forget it. So don't do that.

21

Most of the kids know your heart. They can tell if you truly care about them. They can tell if you're genuine . . . and they respect that authenticity.

22

~~~~~

I imagine there are adults out there who find it challenging to cope with the drama in their own household. Today . . . be mindful of what your students are coping with at home.

23

~~~~~

If you've ever had a bad day, you know how much it means when a colleague picks you up. Sometimes our kids have bad days . . . and we need to pick 'em up. Encouragement never goes out of style.

24

Kids don't want to be bad; they want to have their needs met. It's good when we can focus on understanding the students and meeting their needs . . . rather than just reacting to the "bad behavior."

25

I think students can tell when their teachers enjoy teaching them. At least they think they can. And their perception means everything.

26

~~~~~~

On some days, you may have students who need you to be their cheerleader more than they need you to be their teacher. It's important to remember that some students deal with a lot. And always remember the role you can play in helping them get through it.

27

~~~~~~

Kids want to be heard. Whatever the situation . . . they usually respond better when they feel like their voice has been valued and their experiences have been validated.

28

~~~~~~~

It is hard for many adults to ask their boss for help when they are struggling in their job. We should not be surprised that students are reluctant to ask their teachers for help when they're struggling in school. It's hard for most humans to ask for help.

29

~~~~~~~

We have to care about them as children before we can worry about them as students.

30

Every student wants to be successful. I think this is an important conviction for educators to hold onto as they work to chip away at the barriers to that success. Almost every bad attitude that we perceive can be changed if we can figure out a way to communicate hope.

31

Sometimes strict rules lead to sneaky and rebellious kids. And sometimes they don't. This is because relationships often have a bigger impact on behavior than the rules do.

32

~~~~~

It's good to have high expectations for students. It's great to raise the bar. But here's the thing: those high expectations are actually counterproductive if we do not simultaneously support, encourage, and empower our students to rise to the challenge.

33

~~~~~

We don't always get to pick and choose the moments where we make a difference. We don't always know the conversations that students will remember. As educators, we should never underestimate our impact. We might not know when . . . and we might not know how . . . but our impact is always there.

34

Many years from now there will be adults who share stories about when they were in your class. I hope you never forget that you're helping to shape the future memories of those in your care.

35

Most teachers don't get a lot of attention. Their engaging lessons aren't on Twitter. Their cool interactions with students aren't captured on YouTube. But they're still crushing it. And they're making a difference for a lot of students. I'm grateful for them.

36

Think about the "worst" kids in the school. Many years from now, they may reflect back on their school experience. They'll realize they were challenging. But they may think: "I just wish there had been a teacher who could see my potential and was able to stick with me."

37

When working with students, it's best when we start by focusing on their strengths. It's good for them AND it's good for us.

38

~~~~~~

If we don't get to the root of the misbehavior, it is unlikely that the punishment will solve the problem. Rather than trying to manage kids, it works best when we try to understand them.

39

~~~~~~

How about the student who is continuing to fail every test? How about the student who doesn't have a friend to sit with at lunch? When we look at the school day from the perspective of these students . . . when we take ownership in their struggles, we are on our way to becoming a great school.

40

Your students matter. You already knew that. But never forget that you matter to them.

41

Holding students accountable and demonstrating compassion are not incompatible notions. You can always extend grace while you provide discipline. You can always respect their dignity while you administer consequences.

42

~~~~~~~

I have found that the more I greet students in the hallway, the more they make eye contact with me . . . and the more they initiate a greeting with me the next day. It's usually not that hard to make connections with kids . . . but the adults need to be willing to take the first step.

43

~~~~~~~

There's a lot that we can't control, and there are days when we may feel inadequate . . . but we can always be the reason that a kid smiles.

44

~~~~~

When a student is disrespectful, it is usually not about the teacher. It's usually about the other kids who are watching.

45

~~~~~

Many things that happen during the school day are insignificant to the adults ... but they turn into some big memories for the kids.

46

~~~~~~

The students might not remember how much work you put into your class. But they will always remember how much heart you put into your class.

47

~~~~~~

It's quite possible that the kids you like the least are the ones who need you the most.

48

What if I told you that you're the reason some students come to school? That your smile, your kind word . . . was the highlight of their day?

49

When we act like we're happy to see our students . . . they will end up being happier to see us.

50

~~~~~

Some kids dream of trying to change the world . . . and some are just trying to make it through the day. The best teachers meet the kids right where the kids are.

51

~~~~~

There's at least one thing you need to know about each of your students. I'm not sure what it is—you'll have to get to know them.

52

Students don't usually remember lessons for a long time. But they remember kindness . . . and humor . . . and joy.

53

When adults show up to work . . . happy to be there, they've significantly increased the likelihood that the students will have a great day.

54

~~~~~

When kids misbehave, it's not because they like being in trouble. Good teachers get that. They don't lower the bar; they seek to understand.

55

~~~~~

Teachers don't have to change the world to be heroes. They're heroes when they change the trajectory of a kid's bad day.

56

As a rule of thumb, kids like the teachers who really like them. So it's kind of important to like the kids.

57

Some kids are a bright spot in their teacher's day. And some kids need a teacher to be a bright spot in THEIR day.

58

~~~~~

The most powerful conversation you have with a student . . . you might never remember. But that student will.

59

~~~~~

We can't teach our students responsibility if we don't give them some freedom—some opportunities to let them practice being responsible.

60

~~~~~~

When you understand the power of human connection, you will understand why great teachers get to know their students.

61

~~~~~~

Think about the kids who inspire you to come to work. And think about the fact that you're the reason some kids have a good day.

62

~~~~~~

Teach a kid the course of study, and you're a professional. Teach a kid to think, and you're noble. Ensure a kid feels valued, and you're heroic.

63

~~~~~~

When you ask a student what their favorite class is, their answer usually has nothing to do with the subject . . . it has to do with the teacher.

64

~~~~~~

You need to like all your students. But the ones who annoy you . . . they need to be loved.

65

~~~~~~

Some kids are nervous about going to school today. A smile, a high five, or a quiet conversation could do wonders. The adults in the school matter every day.

66

~~~~~~

When teachers are passionate about their lessons, they can transform the learning. When they are passionate about their students, they can transform the students' lives.

67

~~~~~~

Schools don't change the lives of kids. Individual teachers do.

68

~~~~~~~

Teachers don't need to win over all their students . . . just the ones whom they hope will learn.

69

~~~~~~~

Kids are not complicated. They like to feel supported, encouraged, and valued—same as teachers.

70

It's good to know the content. It's great to know the pedagogy. It's imperative to know the kids.

71

When parents drop their kids off at carpool . . . when they put them on the bus . . . they want to know their kids are walking into a school with adults who will love them and care about their well-being. Test scores are important . . . but that might not be the first thing on a parent's mind.

72

~~~~~

Lots of kids have some really good reasons to have a bad attitude. But we expect them to have a good attitude every day. We should never have higher expectations of the kids than we have of the adults.

73

~~~~~

It's hard for me to conceive of anything more important . . . than helping a student feel valued. And that's one reason relationships are so important. It is through personal connections, that we communicate to them their worth. Our investment in them tells them they matter.

74

A great thing to do . . . is ask the students in the school what they think the adults in the school need to know about them. Listening to what the students have to say . . . and valuing what they have to say . . . goes a long way toward building a great school culture.

75

If you're in need of inspiration, my best advice to you is to talk to some kids. Genuinely get to know them. In my experience, an awareness of how cool they are . . . an understanding of how needy they are . . . reminds me of how important my work is. It motivates me to keep going.

76

~~~~~~~~

Teachers appreciate it when their administrators give them the benefit of the doubt. And that's one thing students always appreciate from their teacher.

77

~~~~~~~~

We do a much better job of teaching our students when we first take the time to understand our students . . . their background, their experiences, their challenges, and their joys.

78

~~~~~~~

Creating a brilliant lesson plan does not count for much if you have not first created a safe space in which students can learn.

79

~~~~~~~

Every kid you teach loves something. They are interested in something. They are nervous about something. They are good at something. I wonder what that something is.

80

You can't control the quality of weekend they just had . . . but you can have a huge impact on their Monday morning. If you work in a school, you will make a difference tomorrow.

81

Some kids are listening to their parents fight this evening. I wonder how that will affect their attitude tomorrow. This stuff matters.

82

~~~~~~

Analyzing the data is important . . . but no one ever made a difference in the life of a spreadsheet. We must remember the kids behind the numbers.

83

~~~~~~

A lot of students come to school with "baggage." The best teachers don't just teach good lessons . . . they understand the "baggage."

84

Kids prefer the teachers who are nice to them. Some things in the school building are not hard to figure out.

85

Teachers appreciate it when students understand what they're teaching. Students appreciate it when teachers understand how they're feeling.

86

~~~~~~

Some kids are hard, they are challenging, and they get on your last nerve. They need you not to give up on them. Their parents do too.

87

~~~~~~

When kids act out, it's usually the result of an unmet need. School punishment may address the behavior, but it doesn't meet the need.

88

The next time you encounter a kid with a challenging behavior, remember there is probably stuff going on at home. This will happen tomorrow.

89

Some kids need extra help with their problems . . . just like some teachers need extra help figuring out how to change their computer login.

90

~~~~~~

Today . . . your kindness to a student could end up being the highlight of their day. Let that sink in for a moment.

91

~~~~~~

Every student wants to be successful. When we find ourselves discouraged by the attitude or the apathy, we should remind ourselves of that.

92

Kids tend to respect teachers who don't take themselves too seriously but take their profession very seriously.

93

We may not raise a test score when we show empathy for a student . . . but our compassion can change a kid's life.

94

~~~~~

For some kids, success is about acing the test. For other kids, success is about finding their smile. All kids are at different places.

95

~~~~~

When we treat kids as they SHOULD be, they become all that they COULD be.

96

Some kids act apathetic. It's an act. Every kid cares about something . . . and we need to figure out what it is.

97

Some stuff that drives the adults crazy, captures the imagination of the kids. We should occasionally look at things from the kids' perspective.

98

~~~~~

Kids are much more likely to remember how you taught and why you taught than what you taught.

99

~~~~~

My own kids have never come home talking about teachers who are creative or innovative. (And these are great things.) But they have consistently talked about teachers who had high expectations, who loved teaching, and who strived to connect with their students.

100

～～～

Teachers, you know you make a difference for kids . . . but never forget the difference you make for the adults. Your support, your collaboration, and your energy . . . it all matters! You make your school a better place to work for your colleagues.

101

～～～

We can't control the home environment of our students, but we can surely control their classroom environment. When they're under our care, they can feel safe, supported, and loved.

102

Building up the confidence of students is more important than building up their knowledge. Content may soon be forgotten, but kids with confidence can change the world.

103

Good teachers don't need Wi-Fi to engage their students. Technology is a great thing . . . but the passion of the teachers is always the most important variable in the classroom.

104

~~~~~~~~

Great teachers make it look easy. . . . but they actually work really hard at it. Greatness never comes without commitment and sacrifice.

105

~~~~~~~~

It's one thing to believe that all children can learn. It's yet another . . . to invest yourself in the success of every child.

106

One of the first steps in connecting with a challenging student . . . is to LIKE them, rather than "put up" with them. It's amazing how the attitude of the adult can affect the attitude of the kid.

107

It doesn't take much to make kids feel special. Look them in the eye. Smile at them. Talk to them individually. Be curious about THEM. Be sincere.

108

Some kids have good smiles; some ask good questions; some are good at magic; some are creative; some are good helpers; some can remember lines from TV shows; some can make kids laugh; some have great handwriting. Every kid can do something well! We need to figure out what it is.

109

Sometimes a student makes bad choices . . . but it doesn't make them a bad kid. I hope we communicate that message to our students. Tomorrow is a new day. (And we're all hoping to be a little bit more mature tomorrow than we were today.)

110

~~~~~~

It is one thing for us to listen to our students. It's yet another . . . for them to feel like they're heard. We can't just tell them that we care about them; they need to FEEL it.

111

~~~~~~

Students are more motivated to learn when their teacher is motivated to teach. Some teachers seem to be going through the motions . . . and some teachers are fired up. Kids recognize the difference. And they are more likely to be inspired by the teachers who are inspired themselves.

112

~~~~~~

You don't have to like all your students . . . just the ones you want to impact.

113

~~~~~~

Sometimes kids make bad choices. Sometimes they really screw up. We hold them accountable . . . but we can also extend some grace. They need to know we still like them. They need to learn a lesson . . . but it is never constructive when they feel alienated from us.

114

～～～

There's a whole bunch of stuff that our students are gonna be thinking about tomorrow other than our lesson. This doesn't mean that we don't teach our hearts out . . . but it means that we ought to be patient; we ought to be empathetic; and we ought to keep things in perspective.

115

～～～

The students don't need you to be perfect . . . but they need you to be involved.

116

~~~~~~~~

Here's something I've noticed about kids: when they feel like you have actually listened to them, the rest of the conversation usually goes much better.

117

~~~~~~~~

Think of your most challenging student. Now imagine that you're their parent. After you finish mumbling to yourself or rolling your eyes, really try to imagine. How much patience would you have? How much potential would you see? At what point would you be willing to give up? Seriously.

118

~~~~~~

Kids don't always follow instructions . . . and neither do teachers. We all need to be patient with one another.

119

~~~~~~

Most of what is true of the kids in the school . . . is also true of the adults. We all feel insecure at times. We all want to be noticed. We all hope to be successful. We all have been hurt by the unkind words of others. We all work harder when friends encourage us.

120

Not all your students come to class wanting to learn . . . but they all come wanting to belong. And when they feel like they belong . . . they're much more likely to learn.

121

When you look at a lesson plan, you will probably not see things like patience, and care, and support, and joy, and a sense of humor . . . yet these are the qualities that define great teachers.

122

~~~~~~~

When you ask the class if they have any questions, and nobody raises their hand . . . that does NOT mean everyone understands.

123

~~~~~~~

It takes courage for teachers to reimagine a classroom different from the one they experienced. I admire those teachers who think outside the box, who challenge the status quo, and who are committed to preparing students for their own future.

124

Connecting with students is not accidental. It only happens when teachers make it a priority. And the good ones make it a priority.

125

When your career is over, you will not remember the lessons or the curriculum maps . . . you will remember the kids and the colleagues. It's the people that matter.

126

~~~~~

The most effective teachers are the ones who realize they're the most important variable in the classroom.

127

~~~~~

Teachers . . . you can be the one whom the "difficult kids" remember . . . the one who was always kind . . . the one who was always patient . . . the one who never gave up on them.

128

The legacy of a great teacher is not built in their lesson plan book . . . but in their conversations with students. The lessons are important . . . but the relationships are essential.

129

Parents are so grateful when they notice teachers demonstrating genuine care for their students. Teachers feel like they are just doing their job, but to the parents . . . that "job" is their whole world.

130

Teachers are more motivated when their administration supports them, values them, and encourages them. Guess when students are more motivated.

131

Reaching the "hard to reach" students is not about having the right strategy . . . it's about having the right heart. It's a passion for connecting with kids.

132

~~~~~~

Teaching is . . . what people do when they want to make a difference . . . when they want to improve the lives of others . . . when they want to create brighter futures . . . when they want to change the world, one child at a time. That's what teaching is.

133

~~~~~~

There are students everywhere . . . who never liked a subject until they got that one special teacher. So it doesn't matter what your subject is . . . you have the potential to be that one special teacher.

134

~~~~~~~~~

We can't ever become so professional that we become callous to what kids deal with. I think the greatest educators hold on to a tender heart.

135

~~~~~~~~~

It's good for adults to talk to kids about values . . . but it's possible those same kids pay closer attention to how the adults behave themselves.

136

There will be times when you invest yourself into a student who desperately needs you . . . and you get burned. Don't be too discouraged. It happens to everyone. And do not be deterred in your commitment to making a difference. We are planting seeds. We don't always see the harvest.

137

I think teachers shine the most . . . not when they're teaching well crafted, innovative lessons . . . but when they're working patiently with students who are struggling.

138

I've noticed teachers are more motivated when they are teaching stuff that interests them. I suspect one of the best ways to motivate kids, is to develop activities that are interesting to THEM. That's not easy . . . but then again, teachers don't become effective by taking it easy.

139

Sometimes teachers have bad days . . . those days when it's hard just walking into the school building in the morning . . . those days when they don't have the energy to get after it . . . those days when they may not even want to talk to people. Kids have those days too.

140

~~~~~

Every time you interact with a student, you have the opportunity to make them feel special. That's some powerful potential that we all have.

141

~~~~~

We teach kids in the classroom . . . but it's a great thing when we acknowledge them outside the classroom. Simply telling them "hello" in the hallway, or giving them a high five after school . . . can remind them that they matter. Don't take that stuff for granted.

142

~~~~~~~~

When you truly listen to students ... they may end up learning more. Listening leads to understanding. Understanding generates compassion. Compassion fosters relationships. Relationships facilitate learning.

143

~~~~~~~~

A lot of kids don't like school. That's the reality. When the adults in the building get to know those kids and genuinely care about them ... they can turn that around. That's also the reality.

144

~~~~~~

Kids go just about anywhere for validation. If you want to connect with a kid . . . find reasons to praise them. We all like hanging around others who make us feel good about ourselves.

145

~~~~~~

When talking to kids . . . don't talk at 'em, over 'em, or down to 'em. They like it when you talk WITH them. I promise you'll get better results.

146

~~~~~~

Students don't know you care about them because you teach them . . . or because you've told them that you do. They know you care about them when you go out of your way to care about them.

147

~~~~~~

Not all kids have the same shot at a successful life. But schools can help level the playing field. Teachers help to level the playing field. You can be one of those teachers who impacts the future of a student and changes a life.

148

~~~~~

Some teachers seem like naturally gifted educators. They may well be . . . but that doesn't mean they don't work really hard at it. People don't just show up exceptional . . . they make a commitment to do whatever it takes . . . to BE exceptional.

149

~~~~~

It's good to teach your students the curriculum, critical thinking, and creative problem-solving. But don't forget to teach your students to have a good handshake, to look people in the eye, and to be considerate of others. In the long run, those things might matter more.

150

~~~~~~

When I think back on my teachers who were most effective, there is something they all had in common: they all seemed excited to be teaching us. Teachers should always be aware of the attitude and energy they bring into class. I promise you, the students are aware of it.

151

~~~~~~

Teaching is not a career for everyone. Not everyone has creativity, and enthusiasm, and flexibility, and compassion, and patience, and perseverance, and composure, and resourcefulness, and passion, and a sense of humor. Nope . . . teaching isn't for everyone.

152

~~~~~~~

The best educators inspire students to think about possibilities. When students are thinking about what COULD be . . . that is when their potential is unleashed.

153

~~~~~~~

We've all benefited from some breaks before. There have been times when someone cut us some slack when we probably didn't deserve it. It's really cool when teachers pay it forward with their students. Kids will remember it.

154

I remember a teacher telling me, "When you're surrounded by superstars . . . it makes you want to be better than you are." That's the power of collaboration—the power of positive peer pressure. The best teachers don't just inspire their students; they inspire their colleagues.

155

In a great classroom, the students aren't the only learners. The TEACHER is a learner also. When teachers are curious, when they are vulnerable, when they continue to grow . . . they provide stronger instruction, and they provide a great example to their students.

156

You can teach an old dog new tricks, and you can teach a veteran teacher new technology. Professional learning is not a function of age . . . it's a function of attitude.

157

It's nice when teachers are creative, dynamic, and innovative . . . but I actually think I prefer patient, flexible, and kind.

158

~~~~~

We talk a lot about students being engaged. It occurs to me that one of the hallmarks of a great classroom is the TEACHER being engaged. Kids love it when their teacher is active, involved, and energized. And they can tell which ones are really "into it" . . . and which ones aren't.

159

~~~~~

I'm inspired by teachers. But it is not usually their lessons that I find inspiring. It is their energy . . . their heart . . . and their passion that fire me up. These teachers make the school a better place just by walking in the door.

160

Good relationships with students usually do not happen accidentally. They are cultivated by great educators intentionally.

161

More than anything else . . . parents want teachers to care about their children. Some qualities are nice to have . . . and some are nonnegotiable. Genuine care is one of those.

162

Teachers don't have to be funny, creative, innovative, inspiring, or charismatic. But they have to care about their students and take pride in their own work. If they do those two . . . they will have a remarkable career.

163

Reflection is one of the keys to success. If it worked, keep it . . . if it sort of worked, tweak it . . . if it bombed, scrap it. Reflection is how we grow. It is how we excel.

164

~~~~~~~~

I appreciate it when teachers correct student behavior without undermining the relationship. Those teachers earn the respect of their students.

165

~~~~~~~~

Teachers enjoy their job more when they allow themselves to have a little fun in the classroom. It turns out that it helps students enjoy the class more too.

166

~~~~~~~~

I think it's a great idea for teachers to ask students for feedback on their class. When they ask in a genuine way, they normally get genuine responses. The goal is for school to be a positive experience, not a painful one.

167

~~~~~~~~

When teachers love their work, the kids know it. When teachers love the kids, they know that too. And the kids usually love those teachers right back.

168

~~~~~~

Some people are inspired by passionate speeches or poignant quotes . . . but to me, there is nothing more inspiring than teachers who are engaged in the hard and meaningful work of educating our children.

169

~~~~~~

Teachers shoulder a greater emotional burden than most people can imagine.

170

The kids in our schools have remarkable talents that are often untapped by traditional curriculum and traditional pedagogy. Props to the teachers who work outside the box in order to create opportunities for ALL their students to thrive.

171

So here's a challenge: think of your most challenging student. Now think of how you might potentially interact with that student differently. I'm not saying their behavior is your fault . . . but sometimes the approach of the adult can be a significant variable.

172

You might have brilliant lessons ... but are you patient with students who need it explained a second or third time? You might utilize all the latest technology ... but do you work with the student who seems to have an attitude? I think these answers matter.

173

I think you'll make more progress with kids when you're trying to build on their strengths instead of just trying to fix their weaknesses.

174

~~~~~~

One of the best things a teacher can do for the students is to find little ways for them to experience success. Success is one of the best motivations there is. It increases the likelihood students will keep working when things get a little tougher.

175

~~~~~~

When a student fails a quiz, or a test, or a project . . . what would compel that student to get it turned around for the next one? I'll tell you one thing: the relentless encouragement and support of a teacher. Props to the teachers who never give up on their students.

176

~~~~~

If you work in a school, you have a reputation there. You might be known for your patience . . . or your enthusiasm . . . or your kindness . . . or your energy . . . or your love of students . . . or your collaboration with colleagues . . . or your innovative lessons. YOU build your reputation.

177

~~~~~

I remember a young teacher asking me for advice as she began her career. My advice was not profound . . . but here it is: learn from your colleagues, don't be afraid to fail, and never stop caring about the kids.

178

~~~~~~~~~

When staff members are having a bad day, how do they hope their principal will deal with them? With grace, with patience . . . cut 'em some slack maybe? When students are having a bad day, how do they hope their teachers will deal with them?

179

~~~~~~~~~

Effective teachers are not naive about their challenges . . . but they focus on what they can control—the quality of their instruction to students and the quality of their interaction with students.

180

~~~~~

The teachers who are the most effective in the classroom are the ones who believe they play the most important role in the learning of their students. They do not view themselves as victims of bad curriculum, "lazy" students, or unsupportive parents. They just get after it!

181

~~~~~

Teachers are not simply raising student achievement; they are in the noble process of developing better humans. Education doesn't just open new doors of personal opportunity; it allows young people to engage their world in a more tolerant, compassionate, and constructive way.

182

~~~~~~~~

You don't just have to hope that your students know that you care about them. You will have an opportunity or two this week to actually show them.

183

~~~~~~~~

The learning environment always influences what is learned. It's never just about the lesson plan.

184

~~~~~~

I think effective teachers are not driven by the standards; they're driven by the needs of their kids. They understand the curriculum and they teach what is required . . . but it's always in the context of understanding where their students are . . . and what it takes to move them.

185

~~~~~~

If you're kind, honest, and a hard worker . . . you'll end up being a great human. The academic standards are important . . . but it's also cool when educators can find ways to reinforce this other stuff.

186

~~~~~~~

Effective instruction involves more than content mastery, pedagogical prowess, and strategic resource utilization. Those three are critical for sure . . . but never underestimate the importance of human connection in the classroom.

187

~~~~~~~

In my experience, teachers like being noticed. It's a very human thing to want to matter. Think about the power educators have to "notice" kids . . . to communicate to them that they matter.

188

Kids appreciate it when you smile at them. They also appreciate you talking to them like a normal person. It doesn't take much to build a connection. But you gotta like 'em.

189

Please remember that all those interactions you have with your students outside of the lesson really matter. The smiles . . . the eye contact . . . the jokes . . . the fist bumps . . . and the silliness . . . they're all important. They remind kids that they matter. Those moments can mean the world.

190

~~~~~~~~~~

There are great teachers who have a "countdown" to summer break. I realize it's a common practice . . . but please think twice about it. You have students who don't want the year to end; they're not looking forward to the summer. Your school is the best place they have.

191

~~~~~~~~~~

Our goal is to make an impact on students. You might not be able to see the difference you're making, but if you are caring about your kids and are committed to doing right by them . . . you ARE making an impact. You ARE making a difference.

192

I think it's brilliant when teachers communicate with parents about the good stuff . . . as opposed to just waiting to drop bombs about the bad stuff. I know it takes time, but I think it's a great investment. It builds relationships with parents, and it cultivates student pride.

193

We need for doctors to know their stuff, but it's also really nice when they have a good "bedside manner." The same if true in the classroom. Teachers need expertise . . . but it's also great when they have a way with kids. I guarantee you it makes a difference to the students.

194

~~~~~~

If you have kids of your own, think about how much you appreciate their teachers who go the extra mile . . . who love them like their own. You can be that teacher for all your students. You're not just making a difference for kids . . . but for a lot of parents too.

195

~~~~~~

I know you go to work for the students . . . but never underestimate the impact you have on your colleagues. Your attitude and your energy can inspire the adults around you to be better than they are. So you can make a difference for kids whom you don't even teach!

196

~~~~~~

The best lesson you teach this year could be ridiculously awesome. The best conversation you have with a student this year could change a life.

197

~~~~~~

When the kids get on your last nerve . . . it's gut check time. It's hard. I know it is. But you've got this! Your patience and compassion make a difference for a lot of students. You've got this!

198

~~~~~~

Teachers don't always feel inspired. They don't always have the passion. They might not always feel like their work matters. But they're professionals . . . and they keep coming to work. And their work DOES matter. EVERY day!

199

~~~~~~

Some of the best professional learning takes place when we solicit feedback from the kids in our class . . . and genuinely listen to it. When we consider the point of view of our students, we significantly increase our potential for making their learning experiences meaningful.

200

~~~~~~

I know you teachers out there have a lot to be thankful for . . . but please remember that there are a lot of parents out there who are thankful for YOU. You often spend more time with their children than they do, and they are grateful for how you teach them, inspire them, and love them.

201

~~~~~~

Teachers don't just inspire students to dream; they give them reasons to hope. And I think the "hope" comes first. It is what makes dreaming possible.

202

Teachers make mistakes; they get sick; they get sad; they get nervous; they get frustrated. As it turns out . . . teachers are human. And this is OK. There can be value in showing some vulnerability in the classroom. It makes teachers "real." And authenticity is always compelling.

203

I love seeing teachers demonstrate professional learning—seeing them look for new ways to engage their students . . . new ways to motivate their students . . . new ways to meet their needs. This professional commitment is the result of a conviction that our kids deserve our best.

204

~~~~~~~~

I think the enthusiasm of the teacher has a bigger impact on student engagement than the lesson itself. Passion can transform any classroom.

205

~~~~~~~~

Genuine care and positive energy are simple things . . . but they are powerful things that are under the control of every teacher. And they have a profound impact on the classroom environment and learning experiences of the students.

206

~~~~~~

Our students notice our mood, notice our attitude, and notice our reactions to adversity. Educators are allowed to be human . . . but it's important to be mindful of the example we set for all the eyes that are watching.

207

~~~~~~

Every heated situation in a school can be diffused or escalated by the adults in the building. Our words, our attitude, our demeanor . . . they all matter.

208

~~~~~~

Lesson plans are important, and pedagogy matters . . . but some of the most important work of teachers might not be captured by a plan. When teachers encourage, support, inspire, care about, and connect with their students . . . they are engaged in work that transcends the "plan."

209

~~~~~~

Sometimes teaching can be a grind. It's not all cute bulletin boards, inspirational lessons, and light bulb moments. But teachers keep going. They persevere in their commitment to engage in meaningful work—to make a difference for students. And I love them for it.

210

~~~~~~

If you notice a successful principal, you should assume there is a faculty of rock stars making the magic happen in the school.

211

~~~~~~

One of the ways to stay motivated in our job is to remain mindful of our purpose. When we are fully aware of how much our students need us . . . how much they need education . . . how much they need someone to care, it is hard not to bring our "A-game."

212

~~~~~~

We don't define our success by our salary, our last promotion, or the zip code of our school. Our success is found in the difference we make for our students and for our colleagues. It's hard to measure, and it's hard to quantify . . . but it's what gives our work true meaning.

213

~~~~~~

Most people don't recall favorite lessons; they recall favorite teachers. The energy and enthusiasm of teachers is what brings lessons to life. Their passion is what is memorable. It is what motivates students to care about their lessons.

214

~~~~~

25 years from now, there will be adults who share your name. They will remember you . . . and they will tell somebody about the difference you made for them. You will be that teacher who made an impact. But right now . . . they're still kids. And you have no idea who they are.

215

~~~~~

The most important qualities of any educator are not adequately captured on a resume. It is hard to quantify passion, energy, dedication, patience, perseverance, and love . . . but in the classroom . . . those qualities make all the difference in the world.

216

I think teachers are best when they are transparent with their passion. Love of content, love of learning, and love of kids . . . is what students find so compelling.

217

The kids in our schools have remarkable talents that are often untapped by traditional curriculum and traditional pedagogy. Thanks to all the teachers who work outside the box in order to create opportunities for ALL their students to thrive.

218

~~~~~

It can be hard to quantify effective teaching. Test scores are certainly not an adequate bottom line. But one thing I know for sure is this: effective teaching is more likely to result from educators who are continually learning and improving their craft.

219

~~~~~

I've noticed that strong teachers don't just have high expectations for their students, they have high expectations for themselves. I think that's one of their secrets.

220

~~~~~

Some educators are exceptional. It is not a fluke, and it's not a mystery. They are passionate about what they do . . . they are passionate about whom they serve . . . and they work their butts off.

221

~~~~~

If students could pick their teachers, would they sign up for your class? I know it's not a popularity contest . . . but the attitude of the teacher always affects the attitude toward the class. And the attitude toward the class always affects the level of learning.

222

~~~~~~

The level of fun that students have in learning is often in direct proportion to the level of fun that their teachers have in teaching.

223

~~~~~~

Great teachers don't plan well to impress their administrators . . . they plan well to engage their students.

224

~~~~~

Teachers who teach kids have an advantage over teachers who teach subjects. They understand the role of personal connections in the process of meaningful learning.

225

~~~~~

I wonder what your students will remember from your class this year. There's a very good chance it won't be a specific lesson. We always need to be mindful of the fact that we're making memories for our kids.

226

~~~~~~

I appreciate empathetic educators. Their job is more stress-ful . . . because they feel the pain and struggles that their students endure. But their job is infinitely more reward-ing . . . because they're the ones who truly touch the lives of their students.

227

~~~~~~

One of the secrets to effective classroom management is holding students accountable in a way that is constructive, and not simply punitive.

228

We earn the respect of our students by how we treat them. It's usually that simple.

229

Teachers aren't perfect . . . and it works best when they don't pretend to be in front of their students.

230

～～～

It's good for students to learn to adjust to their teachers . . . but it's also good for teachers to learn to adjust to their students.

231

～～～

We must expect kids to do the right thing. We intervene if they don't . . . but we don't lower the bar, and we don't lower our expectations.

232

~~~~~~~~

If teachers aren't joyful about teaching . . . there is zero chance the students will be joyful about learning.

233

~~~~~~~~

I know there is a lot of "whole group" instruction that must happen in class . . . but the individual interactions are really where it's at. One-on-one conversations with kids can be so powerful (inside the class and outside the class).

234

~~~~~~

We don't win kids over with consequences; we win them over with relationships. Sometimes, they need conse-quences . . . but we should always be mindful of what it is that will win them over.

235

~~~~~~

Technology has replaced a lot of things in the classroom. It will never replace a smiling teacher . . . greeting kids as they walk into class.

236

Good teachers understand the importance of addressing problem behaviors immediately . . . but they also have the wisdom in knowing which "battles" to fight.

237

Teaching without relationships is sort of like cookies without the chocolate chips. It's possible—it's just not nearly as good.

238

Today, you could be the reason that a student has a great day. You're not just teaching lessons . . . your kindness is making the life of a kid just a little bit easier.

239

When the teacher is in a bad mood, all the kids know it. As it turns out, the teacher is an important variable in the climate of the class.

240

~~~~~~~

When graduates come back to visit teachers, they visit the ones who took an interest in them. If you want to be memorable, take an interest.

241

~~~~~~~

Some adults can think back to a single teacher who didn't give up on them—who helped them get it turned around. You can be that teacher.

242

~~~~

Maintaining high standards of behavior and maintaining positive relationships with your students are not mutually exclusive propositions.

243

~~~~

Sometimes, the most valuable thing educators provide for their students is the structure, stability, and support that they might not get at home.

244

~~~~~~~

If you want to see a teacher's rapport with students, watch them interact with the kids in the hallway. Those interactions speak volumes.

245

~~~~~~~

Just like a successful team has bought into its coach . . . a successful class has bought into its teacher. The relationships matter.

246

~~~~~~

When teachers realize their own attitude affects the motivation of their students . . . it can be a game changer.

247

~~~~~~

Never underestimate the power of high expectations. High expectations for your students . . . and for yourself.

248

~~~~~

I think the best veteran teachers might be the ones who held onto the attitude of a first-year teacher. They want to impact every kid!

249

~~~~~

The single best way for us to teach good character . . . is to model good character. The kids are ALWAYS watching.

250

~~~~~~~~~

It's important that teachers understand the content . . . but it's also important that they understand the kids.

251

~~~~~~~~~

The pace of instructional rigor can never exceed the pace of instructional support.

252

Students are generally more excited about learning when the teacher is excited about teaching. The engagement of the kids is usually connected to the enthusiasm of the adult.

253

Insecure kids are reluctant learners. Teachers should never underestimate the value of encouraging kids . . . of building up their confidence.

254

~~~~~

The teachers who have the biggest impact on kids practice empathy. They don't just teach their students; they try to understand them.

255

~~~~~

The best classroom management plan has always been and always will be . . . a good lesson.

256

~~~~~~

Professional development should not be about a workshop, class, or activity. It's a mindset. It's a relentless pursuit of being better tomorrow than you were today.

257

~~~~~~

Kids appreciate teachers who don't take themselves too seriously. A little vulnerability from the teacher goes a long way in building class climate.

258

~~~~~~~~

Educators who are extraordinary became that way by making lots of little decisions to rise above mediocrity.

259

~~~~~~~~

Teachers have the ability to give students something that is far more valuable than good grades on a report card. They can give them hope.

260

~~~~~~

Teachers want their administrators to support them, to validate them, and to inspire them. Guess what students want from their teachers . . .

261

~~~~~~

Teachers like professional learning that is relevant, engaging, safe, and in a comfortable environment. Guess what kind of learning students like . . .

262

~~~~~~

When teachers decide to have a good day, their students often end up having a good day as well.

263

~~~~~~

Good teaching is not accidental. It results from teachers who plan well and connect with their students. Both of these are intentional.

264

~~~~~

I remember a teacher telling me: "It'll be ok. And if it doesn't work, we'll do it differently next year." Attitudes like that are a blessing to a principal . . . and to a school.

265

~~~~~

The positive energy of the teacher is the single most important factor in determining the climate of the classroom.

266

~~~~~~

Good teaching is not just delivering lessons. It's about being invested in the success of your students. It's a commitment to the kids.

267

~~~~~~

When teachers give students hope . . . when they inspire them to envision a life that can be different . . . then they are heroes.

268

You never know the impact you are having on a kid. Keep encouraging, keep supporting, keep loving—even when they don't seem to care.

269

It's hard to teach a good lesson without a plan. But a good lesson plan does not necessarily make for good teaching.

270

~~~~~~

When teachers deliver good lessons, they are professionals. When they brighten the day of hurting kids, they are
heroes.

271

~~~~~~

One of the greatest things teachers can do for their students
is to instill in them the belief that they can do more than
they ever imagined.

272

~~~~~~~~

If teachers are determined to make a difference with kids, they will. That's the beauty of the right attitude. Our purpose is everything.

273

~~~~~~~~

No kid likes being in trouble; no kid likes failing; and no kid wants to be labeled a "loser." We need to remember that.

274

~~~

Sometimes, it's important for kids to see their teacher make mistakes . . . to see them modeling the process of overcoming failure.

275

~~~

All teachers face challenging students. An average teacher gets discouraged. A great teacher gets their circumstances, gets their potential, gets busy, and gets to make a difference.

276

～～～～

Three things students want from their teachers: to enjoy their job; to be excited about the lesson; and to love the kids.

277

～～～～

Most kids don't realize how much potential they have. That's where teachers come in. They inspire students with possibilities.

278

~~~~~~~

The best teachers are not driven by courses of study . . . they are driven by the faces in front of them.

279

~~~~~~~

When teachers focus on skill acquisition rather than content memorization, they make themselves more relevant—and their students more engaged.

280

~~~~~~

Being a great teacher is hard work. They make it look effortless in the classroom, but a great deal of effort goes into it.

281

~~~~~~

As it turns out, the first important step in effective classroom management . . . is actually liking the kids in your classroom.

282

Resources are good; pedagogy is good; but never underestimate the human element. Teachers are the most important variable in the classroom.

283

A good lesson plan is no substitute for a good teacher.

284

~~~~~

Good teachers can look past the bad attitude. They realize there's always something else going on.

285

~~~~~

All teachers have bad days. Great teachers keep things in perspective . . . and always do right by kids.

286

While policy makers are trying to change curriculum, text-books, and assessments . . . teachers are trying to change lives.

287

Kids aren't inspired by lessons . . . but by teachers—teachers who bring joy to the room, passion for their subject, and love for the students.

288

Great teachers are always in pursuit of a better lesson. They demand the same excellence from themselves that they hope for in their kids.

289

Effective classrooms are not the result of smart, well behaved kids . . . but of teachers planning good lessons and getting to know their students.

290

~~~~~~~~

The unwritten expectations of the teacher are always more powerful than the written rules posted on the wall.

291

~~~~~~~~

The best teachers don't always have the best lessons, but they always have the best relationships with kids.

292

~~~~~~

Developing the right classroom climate is always more important than developing the right lesson. But great teachers are committed to both.

293

~~~~~~

Principals don't need all their teachers to be innovative . . . but they need all of them to be team players, to love kids, and to stay positive.

294

~~~~~

If your student forgets his pencil, give him a pencil. Don't make a thing of it. There are better ways to teach responsibility.

295

~~~~~

Teachers can prepare kids for the test without building relationships with them—but the test is not the ultimate goal of a good teacher.

296

The golden rule for educators: teach every child the way you would want your own child to be taught.

297

The challenge for teachers is not to increase their students' capacity for knowing . . . but to increase their capacity for DOING.

298

~~~~~~~~~~

It's not about having the right gift, or the right skill, or the right talent. It's about having the right heart.

299

~~~~~~~~~~

If you're positive, passionate, and persistent . . . you WILL make a difference.

300

Lots of adults wake up and go to jobs. JOBS. Teachers wake up and have the chance to change lives. It is a passion and a privilege.

301

Good teachers are not intent on winning "battles" with the students. They know that if there is a battle in the classroom, nobody wins.

302

~~~~~~

Instruction without rigor is weak. Instruction without relevance is lame. Instruction without relationships is futile.

303

~~~~~~

The most valuable contribution of a teacher might not be found in helping a student excel, but in helping a student work through failure.

304

One of the most important things educators can do is create a safe environment. Growth only happens in the context of vulnerability.

305

Teachers are not successful because they have the right curriculum, the right lesson plan, or the right resources. They are successful because they have the right mindset.

306

~~~~~~~~

Teachers are not defined by their lesson plans. They are defined by their passion.

307

~~~~~~~~

There is not one magical instructional strategy . . . but there is magic in connecting with kids.

308

~~~~~~~~

Too many teachers give too many answers to students who don't have the questions. The best teachers cultivate curiosity.

309

~~~~~~~~

Getting to work on time, getting their grades posted, calling parents, ensuring their students are always supervised, maintaining student confidentiality—it's not just about the lessons. I appreciate teachers who take care of the other stuff too . . . because they're professionals.

310

~~~~~

You don't have to do a TikTok for them. You don't have to rap for them. You don't have to be a comedian for them. And you don't need a creative handshake for every one of them. Just take pride in your teaching, genuinely care, and be committed to the success of every student.

311

~~~~~

There are some teachers down the hall who have some awesome ideas . . . that need to be stolen. That's what good teachers do . . . steal awesome ideas wherever they can find them.

312

~~~~~~~~

Our commitment to professional growth must always override our desire to remain comfortable.

313

~~~~~~~~

When someone gives you the benefit of the doubt . . . you will be thankful. Don't forget to pay it forward. That is something that everyone appreciates.

314

~~~~~

You don't need anyone's permission to be awesome.

315

~~~~~

We want our students to feel like they're amazing . . . with so much to offer the world. Well—it starts with us! We need an abiding conviction that WE are amazing . . . with so much to offer the world. We can give what we don't have.

316

~~~~~

We all give off vibes . . . and these vibes impact those around us. It is inescapable. Sometimes our influence is intentional, and sometimes it is accidental. But be assured . . . we are always making an impact.

317

~~~~~

There were educators over the course of my career who helped me. They didn't have to; there was nothing in it for them, but they made a difference for me . . . and I'm grateful. We all have experienced that before . . . and we all can pay it forward with our kids and colleagues.

318

~~~

Sometimes students are uncooperative. Sometimes our colleagues are aggravating. Sometimes the parents don't support us. Sometimes the "tests" discourage us. Sometimes the "policies" undermine us. We can't control it. So we push on. We focus on making a difference for the KIDS!

319

~~~

When you are slow to judge and quick to listen . . . when you assume the best intentions of your colleagues . . . you make yourself a great team player. And you single-handedly play a role in elevating the morale of the faculty.

320

~~~~~~

The vast majority of parents are on our side. They just want to be communicated with. We all want the same thing . . . what's best for their kids.

321

~~~~~~

Maslow's "hierarchy of needs" explains some of the dynamics in a classroom, and it's essential to understand this for classroom management. It explains why embarrassing students often leads to disrespectful behavior.

322

~~~

Some kids have drama at home, drama on the bus, and drama in the hall. It's great when classrooms can be a safe haven for kids.

323

~~~

One of my favorite things about school culture . . . is that everyone gets to contribute to it. It is not just a reflection of the administration or the leadership team; it is a reflection of everyone.

324

~~~~~~~

What you believe about why you go to work each day really does matter. It affects your motivation, your dedication, and your gratification. It's a good idea to remind yourself from time to time . . . about why you do what you do.

325

~~~~~~~

There will be circumstances this year that are out of your control. But this year, you will have the potential to impact a child's life. And you can always control what you do with that potential.

326

~~~~~

The greatest joy is not found in our ability to improve our own life . . . but in our ability to improve the lives of others.

327

~~~~~

Some of your colleagues might seem like they have it all together. They don't. Everyone has struggles. Everyone is dealing with stuff. And everyone appreciates kindness.

328

Never underestimate your ability to have a good day on purpose.

329

I don't always have enthusiasm. And I don't always feel passion. But . . . I can always choose to be patient, I can always choose to be kind, and I can always choose to be compassionate. You don't have to be victims of our emotions. Never forget . . . you always make choices.

330

~~~~~

Educators who are more preoccupied with giving respect, than getting respect . . . end up getting more respect.

331

~~~~~

You may have an eloquently crafted philosophy of education. You may have developed a killer resume. But what I'm much more interested in . . . is how you treat the students who might seem unlovable . . . and how you respond to your colleague who needs assistance.

332

~~~~~

When you work hard, when you are nice to others, and when you demonstrate integrity . . . you are a great role model for your students.

333

~~~~~

We can't control the funding, the mandates, or the parents. But . . . we CAN control the energy we bring every day! We CAN control the passion we bring for changing the lives of our students! Our commitment to THESE things is how we impact our culture.

334

~~~~~~

You have a better chance of cultivating the critical thinking when you have first cultivated the critical relationships.

335

~~~~~~

Some of the best professional learning takes place when you're hanging out with the teacher down the hall. Workshops and conferences are nice ... but they will never replace meaningful collaboration within the school.

336

Our thoughts matter. They can shape how we feel and shape how we behave. So it's a good habit to think regularly about the things that really matter to us. The more we reflect on what we truly care about, the more consistently we will live out our values.

337

At a bare minimum, we should expect of ourselves what we expect of our students . . . in terms of work ethic, attitude, and commitment.

338

~~~

Sometimes, school is hard . . . for the kids AND the adults. Teachers deal with all sorts of challenges . . . from over-crowding to unruly kids to difficult parents. Staff members who rise above the adversity and remain positive are leaders . . . and they have a huge impact on the culture.

339

~~~

We all know there are students who are lonely. But it's also possible that we have colleagues who are lonely. There may be staff members who don't feel part of the "family" about which it's so easy to talk. We all can do a better job of paying attention to the adults around us.

340

~~~~~

We can't do anything about last week. We don't know what tomorrow holds. But we have today . . . and we can crush it.

341

~~~~~

You're gonna make mistakes this year. That's ok . . . you'll learn from them. They'll make you better. Don't be afraid of mistakes; embrace the process.

342

We can use our words to tear down or to build up. We can use them to hurt or to heal. Our words are powerful. Our students notice them, and so do our colleagues.

343

We want our students to have a good attitude . . . to persevere . . . to work with pride . . . to overcome adversity . . . to work well with others . . . and to strive for excellence. It starts with us.

344

~~~~

Here are four ways to be a good colleague:

1) Give the adults around you the benefit of the doubt.
2) Focus on solutions rather than dwelling on negativity.
3) Model a relentless commitment to doing right by kids.
4) Be willing to stand in the gap when your colleague needs help.

345

~~~~

I believe inspiration is born out of an abiding conviction about the value of one's work. When you feel like your tank is empty, and you're running on fumes . . . remember the impact you are having on students; remember the encouragement you are providing to colleagues. Your work matters!

346

~~~~~~~

Your best work is in front of you. Seriously. Think about that. And if that's not your mindset, it might be time to hang it up.

347

~~~~~~~

You don't have to be an administrator, grade level chair, or department head to be a leader in your school. Your title doesn't matter. You just have to care about making it better. Passion and commitment can transform any culture.

348

~~~~

Make time for shenanigans at work. Silliness reduces stress, elevates morale, and makes us all a bit more human.

349

~~~~

Students will remember your attitude longer than they will remember your lesson. We better bring a good one every day.

350

~~~~~~

You never know when your passion is inspiring someone around you . . . so keep bringin' it!

351

~~~~~~

As educators, we should be an example to our students. We should read; we should be curious; we should learn and continue to grow; we should open ourselves up to new ideas. If we see the world in exactly the same way we did 5 years ago, we're not doing it right.

352

~~~~~

We are preparing students to be successful . . . but we also need to prepare them to fail. Life is not easy. We need to teach students how to overcome adversity.

353

~~~~~

One of the greatest lessons we can teach our kids is the importance of making sacrifices to reach our goals. Success does not usually come without hard work.

354

~~~~~~

Some students don't have a lot of hope. That's where education comes in; that's the power of teachers. They offer hope.

355

~~~~~~

Great educators are not defined by the test scores they generate or the programs they implement. I think their greatness is found in the hundreds of little interactions that they have with students every day. They are what will be remembered. They are what make a difference for kids.

356

~~~~~

The future does not belong to the 'educated' ... but to those who continue to learn. Creating independent learners is our awesome challenge.

357

~~~~~

The best education does not prepare students for a test ... or for a college ... or for a job. It prepares them to keep learning.

358

The best lessons are not taught, they are lived. The adults in the school need to remember that the kids are always watching.

359

Our educational practices should not be grounded in tradition; they should be grounded in what the research says is best for students. This is the difference between a job and a profession.

360

~~~~~~

Education isn't a goal, and it isn't a thing that kids obtain. It's a process that should give young people hope and a sense of empowerment to create for themselves the future that they want.

361

~~~~~~

Teachers want to know how to motivate students who don't care. One of my thoughts is to care about students who aren't motivated. I realize it's not always that simple. But teachers should never underestimate the value of genuine care.

362

~~~~~~

Educators like to attend conferences where they come away feeling good about who they are, what they do, and what their potential is. Those are the types of classrooms that kids like to attend too.

363

~~~~~~

Great classroom management is not about controlling the behavior; it's about winning over the kids.

364

~~~~~

If you want to know what good teaching looks like, ask some students.

365

~~~~~

We wake up . . . we go to work . . . we are kind to those around us . . . we come home and love our family. We make our little corner of the world a better place because we are here. That's what we do.

Index of Quotes by Topic

Printed in the United States
by Baker & Taylor Publisher Services